The Malachite Bed

and other
SELECTED SHORTS

Harriett Bley

Copyright ©2007 Harriett Bley

ISBN 0-9771042-3-0

Printed in
Ithaca, New York

Published by
The WORDPRO Press
410 E. Upland Rd
Ithaca, NY 14850

Printed on acid free paper.

Aknowledgements

I am indebted to my friends and mentors of
THE INTERNATIONAL WOMEN'S WRITING
GUILD
who for many years have guided and encouraged
me to write and to read my stories at the annual
conferences held at Skidmore College

* * * * *

I also thank my friends in Ithaca who write with me
on Wednesday mornings
under the skillful promptings of
Irene Zahava

These stories are for my daughter, Jane, who makes me wonder where she ever learned to be such a wonderful mother.

For my son, Jonathan, who once said that some of the best times of his life were spent with me, as well as some of the worst.

For my husband, Hy, who if he were given to expressing such feelings, would undoubtedly agree with Jonathan.

And for Julia and Esther who I hope are learning from me how to be a loving Grandmother.

Contents

* * * * *

1	The Malachite Bed
4	Celebration
6	The Quilter's Tale
10	Cherry Picker
13	The Queen and I
16	Home Improvements, 1933
18	The Cabbage
20	What She Did for Love
22	Running with Lollipops
23	A Material Girl
24	School Shoes
26	Party Shoes
27	Skating Shoes
28	Bookmobile
31	B Is for Bellybutton
32	Dress Up
34	The Devines
35	Tea Party
36	Playing in Traffic
38	Two in a Tub
40	Crayolas
42	Sliced White Bread
44	Sunday Visits
46	Lilacs to Brooklyn
49	One Sunday Afternoon
50	Why I Live Over The Moosewood Restaurant

The Malachite Bed

Moments after I am mugged, I lie stunned and bruised on the sidewalk in front of a Love Drugstore with those Love soap bubbles dancing about my head. I reach for an orange that was knocked out of my shopping bag, and a passerby retrieves a head of lettuce. Someone says how lucky I am, that after all, only a few dollars were taken, and I'm not badly hurt, just shaken up a bit. I don't feel lucky. Once again I have been mugged in broad daylight on a busy street in my own neighborhood. Painfully I gather my packages, smooth down my clothing, and slowly start towards home.

At my corner, in the window of a new furniture store, I see a bed that stops me dead in my tracks. The king sized headboard is green malachite formica shaped like a a fully unfurled peacock tail. The eyes of the tail are lit with miniature blue and green twinkling lights. Never have I seen, nor could I have imagined, such a bed. It is awesome and I am seduced.

I enter the store and a salesman approaches, eager to point out the features of this amazing bed. I learn that the headboard conceals hidden compartments and shelves and all sorts of secret storage places. There is a built in stereo system and at the press of a button, a TV screen surfaces into position from the base of the bed. The salesman shows me how the head and the foot of the mattress can be raised or lowered for maximum comfort. He invites me to lie down so he can demonstrate the built-in oscillating massage system. I don't have to be asked twice. Penetrating warmth eases my tired muscles while rollers work up and down my spine soothing all of the vital acupuncture pressure points. The salesman informs me that there are forty-four of these points in the human body. I ache in all of them. He points out an electronic panel with outlets for a voice activated computer, a video phone, a halogen reading lamp and a 911 Panic Button that connects directly to the 24th precinct And finally, he draws my attention to a digital sound panel that induces sleep with synthesized sounds of the natural environment: ocean surf, rainfall, murmuring pines, bird calls, or the chirping of crickets in late summer meadows.

"As you can see," says the salesman, This bed comes equipped with every convenience. It takes care of all your needs."

"My God," I think, "he's right! A person could live in a bed like this."

I buy it.

I have had all the furniture in my apartment removed, and when the bed is delivered it fills the room wall to wall. It is resplendent; an island, a safe haven. I long to sink into it, to stretch out and luxuriate in a gentle massage to my neck and shoulders. But first there are some details that I must attend to. I make a hasty trip downtown to *Bed Bath and Beyond* where I find a king-size sheet and comforter set in a 600 thread count cotton *malachite* print! I buy four sheets for window curtains and one for a shower curtain, and an extra pillow case to cover my dachshund's bed. I am Intrigued by this developing malachite theme. I stop at *Ultra Vision* where I had recently admired a pair of malachite eyeglass frames. In less than an hour, as the ads promise, I emerge with my lenses fitted into the malachite frames. I am pleased. I like a coordinated look.

Back in my apartment, I write a letter to my sister in West Palm Beach telling her that I will not be joining her in her *Happy Days Condo Village*. And then I write to the renting agent. For years he has been after me to move so he could raise the rent on my sweet little rent controlled nest. Now, in a flourish of green ink, I inform him that I am renewing my lease.

It is two weeks since I moved into my malachite bed. I subscribe to *Gourmet Meals on Wheels*. On weekends, and sometimes late at night, I phone out for something Indian, Greek, or Tex-Mex. Sundays at 4:00 P.M.I listen to *Selected Shorts*. If I doze off during a story, I tune in at six o'clock and listen on the A.M. station. I have opened a charge account with a Home Shopping Channel that features a program once a month called Malachite at Midnight, and from the coziness of my bed, I buy many coordinated items.

Now when the Wild Man of 96th St. terrifies the neighborhood, or when bullets fly beneath my window as bank robbers shoot it out with the police, I watch it happen on the West Side Cable Channel. I turn on the gentle massage, I select a program of electronic meadow patterns, and to the sound of chirping crickets and a running brook, high above the turbulent streets, I am lulled to sleep in my wonderful malachite bed.

Under the title "A Bed for All Seasons" this story won first prize in a contest sponsored by "Selected Shorts" at Symphony Space in New York City. It was read by Linda Lavin over National Public Radio and has become known as
THE MALACHITE BED

Celebration

Every day during the summer of 1945, I sat on a high stool at a long table in Uncle Reuben's shirt factory snipping khaki colored threads from army jackets and checking for missing buttons. As a child, I had loved going to the factory. Uncle Reuben let me rummage through the trash bins for scraps of cloth to take home with me. Grandma showed me how to use a teacup for a pattern and cut out circles and gather them around the edges into Yo-Yos to make coverlets for my dolls. I sewed little squares of chambray to squares of oxford cloth and discovered the Nine Patch! And under grandma's watchful eye, I sewed Log Cabin and Maple Leaf quilt blocks, and learned to embroider all those beautiful stitches to use on Crazy Quilts.

That summer Uncle Reuben was making shirts for Uncle Sam. There were no lovely scraps of material for me at the factory. Government specifications did not allow for waste, and at the end of the work day, only bits of khaki material remained to be swept up into the dumpsters. I craved bright colors and interesting patterns. Life was drab enough with gas rationing and shoe rationing. I was tired of meatless days and substitutes for sugar and butter. In September I would have to postpone college and work in the factory full time. I had two cousins fighting somewhere in the Pacific who also couldn't finish college. As my fingers mechanically snipped away at khaki threads, I prayed that the war would end, and I dreamed of the glorious quilts that I would make when the world was at peace.

At noon on August 14, I was sitting at the long table, snipping and stitching, when a great shout arose from below.

THE WAR IS OVER! JAPAN HAS SURRENDERED!

We ran to the windows. The street was in an uproar with people shouting, horns blaring, church bells ringing. Someone started singing *God Bless America* and I joined in with tears streaming down my cheeks. From the opened windows of every building up and down Seventh Avenue, tons of confetti and streamers of toilet paper came spiraling down. And the garment district, caught up in the delirium of victory, were flinging out scraps and lengths of fabric. I leaned far out and caught a shimmering ribbon of cloth as it drifted down.

Realizing what had to be done, I went into action. I overturned two large cartons of khaki colored cloth and dragged them to the elevator. It seemed to take forever to get down to street level, but finally, I joined the jubilant crowds. I stumbled as a strip of cloth wrapped around my ankles. Fabric lay everywhere. I was walking on silk, on satin, on crushed velvet. I was walking on air! I stood dazed for just a moment, and then amidst the joyous shouting and dizzying swirls of cloth, I began stuffing the cartons.

This story appeared in "THREADS" magazine during the fifty year anniversary of the end of World War II

The Quilter's Tale

There once was a Quilter who lived in an apartment high above the teeming streets in the garment district of a large industrial city. After dark, when the sewing machines were shut down and the factories were silent, the Quilter laced up her Magic Balance Sneakers and ventured down into the deserted alleys where she rummaged in the dumpsters that were waiting to be picked up by the garbage trucks. There among the sweepings, she found pieces of cloth that were so beautiful that she squealed with delight as she stuffed each piece into her Big Brown shopping bag. To this Quilter, the motto, ***The One Who Dies With The Most Fabric Wins***, was not just a bumper sticker, it was a way of life.

Throughout the years, she had filled every nook and cranny of her small apartment with fabric. Her kitchen cabinets held sun prints and hand dyed indigos. The coat closet was filled with batiks, mud cloth, and wax prints. The medicine cabinet was stuffed with fat quarters; the shower stall was piled with remnants from Marimekko, Hoffman, and Liberty of London. Under her bed she hoarded Japanese sashiko cloth and material from antique kimonos. Instead of drinking water from the kitchen faucet, she quenched her thirst with a mixture of nectar and marigold petals, and instead of using tap water to bathe, she cleansed her body with bee pollen and herbs. This freed up the kitchen sink and the bath tub, giving her ever more room to add to her stash of fabric.

One dark night, the Quilter was searching in a dumpster at the darkest end of a dark alley when suddenly, the piece of cloth that she was about to stuff into her shopping bag was snatched right out of her hands, and a voice growled, "Beat it! This stuff is mine! This dumpster is mine!"

The Quilter dropped her shopping bag, spilling the treasures that she had gathered, and lickety split, her Magic Balance Sneakers carried her back to the safety of her apartment. Exhausted and gasping for breath, she slipped into a troubled sleep. She dreamed that a Bird of Many Colors enfolded her in its wings and rocked her gently. When she was calm, the bird said, 'Sew some fabric into a quilt and I will take it down to the man in the dumpster, for it has begun to snow and he shivers with the cold." The Quilter did as the bird requested. All night long she cut and pieced and stitched. When morning came, the quilt was finished, and the bird carried it down to the dumpster and covered the man who lived there. And he was no longer cold..

The next night The Bird of Many Colors again appeared on The Quilter's windowsill. He was flapping his wings excitedly and his voice was hoarse and urgent. "There is a large room in the city hospital filled with cribs in which infants flail about and cry day and night for they were born addicted to drugs and they must endure the agonies of withdrawal. The Quilter didn't even wait to be asked. She sewed dozens of soft, cuddly quilts appliqued with teddy bears and kitty cats. And when The Bird of Many Colors carried the quilts down and wrapped each baby in his own blankey, the screams subsided and the infants slept.

When The Bird of Many Colors next appeared on The Quilter's window ledge, he was greatly agitated, hopping back and forth. "There has been an earthquake," he croaked. In a far off country thousands of people have perished and thousands are homeless and distraught. Make as many quilts as quickly as you can for these people have lost everything. The Quilter felt the pain of those stricken people. She worked day and night making many quilts and The Bird of Many Colors carried the quilts to the people of that devastated country who knew that others cared. And they were comforted.

Still The Bird of Many Colors came demanding more and more quilts; for a man who huddled for warmth over a sidewalk grating, for a child recovering from the effects of chemotherapy, for mothers in welfare hotels, for battered women in shelters, for victims of hurricanes and floods. The Quilter made as many quilts as The Bird of Many Colors requested. She sewed day and night growing ever more weary. After all, she was no spring chicken. Her bones lacked density. Her blood pressure was high and her bad cholesterol far exceeded her good cholesterol. She complained to The Bird of Many Colors that she could no longer see to thread the needle. "Look," she said holding up the quilt that she had just finished. "See how large and uneven the stitches are?" Do you see how the points don't meet, how the corners don't match?"

"Not to worry," said The Bird of Many Colors. "From a galloping horse, those corners would never be noticed. Anyway, finished is better than perfect." And off he flew with the quilt of the uneven stitches and the mismatched corners. He tucked it gently around a boy who was spending his first night in yet another foster home. And the boy stopped sobbing and was comforted.

Now The Quilter's stash of fabric was just about used up. Even the threads and snippets had been gathered by The Bird of Many Colors and dropped over the trees in the little park for the birds to use in building their nests. The Quilter lamented that just a few pieces of cloth remained. She had never gotten around to making the quilt of her dreams, her masterpiece. "And now my eyes are clouded and my fingers are stiff. "I should have made it sooner," she sighed.

"Do not worry, " said The Bird of Many Colors. Tenderly he wrapped her in his wings and called forth three tiny spiders that lived in the bonsai forest on the window ledge. And the spiders sewed the last pieces of cloth into a quilt that shimmered with stars. The stitches were tiny and evenly spaced. The points matched perfectly. It was a masterpiece.

The Bird of Many Colors covered The Quilter with the beautiful, perfect quilt. And she was content. For now she knew that it is not the one who dies with the most fabric who wins, but the one who uses up the most fabric during her lifetime to comfort others.

Cherry Picker

When they asked what she wanted for her seventieth birthday, she tried to look surprised, as though she had never given it the slightest thought. Actually, she knew exactly what she wanted. She had wondered when they would get around to asking.

"So you want to know what I want for my birthday? What I *really* want?

"Yes, Mother, we want to know what you really want. We want to get you something special that you really want."

"Well," she said, "now that you ask, I'll tell you."

She spoke slowly, emphasizing each word. "What I want is a cherry picker." Startled, the daughters looked at each other as their mother continued. "I've been thinking about it for some time. I want one of those tall machines that they use when they fix the telephone wires, c*herry pickers*, that's what they're called, isn't it?"

Her daughters shook their heads sadly. She had seen that look on their faces before. It was the look that said,

"This time, mother has really gone off the deep end."

She hadn't meant to alarm them, so she added hastily,

"You wouldn't have to buy it. I'm sure it is possible to rent a cherry picker just for a few hours."

"Be serious, Mother. We want to get you something really nice for your seventieth birthday."

They had a birthday feast sent in from a Chinese restaurant. They presented her with a group picture of all the grandchildren framed in sterling silver. They gave her a pillow filled with buckwheat husks that would conform to the shape of her neck and a flowered down comforter with sheets and pillow cases to match. "And look at these, Mother," said the younger daughter, holding up a pair of

fluffy slippers. "You're going to love these. What you do is, you warm these little packets of scented herbs in the microwave and slip them into the linings of the slippers before you put the m on. You can even wear them to bed and enjoy therapeutic heat and aroma therapy while you sleep. You'll enjoy that, won't you? "
"Yes, dear, I am sure I will. I will enjoy every one of your lovely presents. It was wonderful having you all here together, a real treat. And the dumplings"--- She put the fingers of her right hand to her lips and blew a kiss--- "the dumplings were delicious!"

The grandchildren hugged her. Her son kissed her on both cheeks, The daughters went into the bedroom to make up her bed with the new flowered linens. They warmed the herb packets in the microwave and slipped their mother's feet into the fragrant slippers. They tucked her under the flowered quilt and made sure that her head rested comfortably on the buckwheat pillow. "Good night, Mother," they whispered, "Sleep tight. Pleasant dreams."

It is quiet. A delicious aroma of cinnamon, cloves, and eucalyptus enfolds her. She is relaxed, she floats. Pigeons pass beneath her. Clouds drift above. She is standing in the bucket of a yellow cherry picker. Through the headphones that are attached to her yellow hard hat, she speaks to the driver below. "Stop. Come in closer to the building. I want to wash my windows." She hears beeping sounds that indicate that the driver is backing up. When the cherry picker is in position, she uses a long handled mop to scrub the grimy panes of her living room windows, and for good measure, she scrapes the pigeon droppings off the ledges She leans far out and sets free a yellow happy face Frisbee that had been lodged in the baroque masonry of the window cornice since last spring. That accomplished, she tells the driver to move out over the curb. "Go slowly," she instructs, "Those ginko trees need pruning." As they continue down the street, she lops off scraggly tree limbs and releases flocks of plastic bags that had been trapped in the branches by the wind. She watches with pleasure as the bags waft down to the pavement. At the corner, she performs several tricky maneuvers with the mop handle and succeeds in lifting a pair of faded sneakers that had been dangling by their laces from the arm of the lamp post. She smiles when they land with a satisfying thud on the sidewalk below.

Standing in the bucket of the cherry picker, she has an unobstructed view of a brilliant sunset that is spangling the buildings and water tanks with gold. From the windows of her apartment, she barely sees the sky, no less such a glorious sunset. She breathes it in like a tonic. She is elated. She could sprout wings and fly off over the river, over the rainbow, like those happy little bluebirds in the Judy Garland song. *Birds fly over the rainbow, Why then, oh why, can't I?* The words to the song come to her, and she sings them aloud as she watches the sun disappear beyond the river.

Finally, she tips the yellow hard hat back on her head, and calls down to the driver that she is ready to go home. As the cherry picker lurches forward, the mop pail overturns, splashing stars against the darkening sky, in celebration of her seventieth birthday.

The Queen and I

It kills me to think that I am the same age as Queen Elizabeth of England.. Could any two lives be less alike? I mentioned this to my therapist. He told me to pretend that I *was* Queen Elizabeth. He said that pretending that I wore a crown would help me to stand up taller, to smile more often, to be more assertive, and to appear more gracious. I did as he suggested. I smiled when I washed the dishes, I stood up straight when I vacuumed, I was gracious and assertive when I took out the garbage. But my crown went unnoticed. My husband wanted to know if I had a stiff neck.

Actually, there are times when my husband could act more regally towards me. At the mall, for example. He doesn't have to walk three steps behind, I just want him to stay at my side and not go dashing off into Radio Shack while I am still checking things out at The Gap. I find it disconcerting when comments meant for his ears end up in the ears of perfect strangers.

At any rate, it is far-fetched to imagine Queen Elizabeth at a shopping mall, with or without her husband. As far as I can gather from TV, Prince Philip does not often accompany her at garden parties, either. On such occasions, The Queen stands alone, wearing a large brimmed hat and a flowered gown, the handles of her handbag dangling from the crook of her elbow. She smiles the smile reserved for garden parties, and she nibbles a strawberry or two, but all in all, she does not seem delighted to be there.. At the most recent backyard party that I attended, I wore blue jeans and flip flops and consumed a generous amount of cold beer and pizza. If there had been TV coverage, it would have been apparent that I was having a very good time.

The Queen has two birthdays. She was born on April 21, but April in London is cold and damp. In order to have perfect weather for the festivities, the royal birthday is officially celebrated on June 17. For what is so rare as a day in June? I was born in February, and I still remember with regret, how two or three birthday parties of my childhood had to be called off because of blizzards. I'm sure my therapist would approve if I acted assertively and proclaimed an official June birthday for myself. Which I hereby do.

By the way, what do you give a Queen for her birthday? For several years when we were newly married, my husband, still romantically inclined, gave me Hamilton Beach kitchen appliances to mark significant occasions. He thought I would appreciate having my initials, HB, inscribed right there on the handle of the fry pan, and on the rim of the crock pot. I wonder if the Queen's kitchen appliances are engraved with her initials? I read that she likes to relax at Balmoral Castle and dabble in the kitchen. Does she have a platinum potato peeler, a sterling silver salad spinner?

A very important duty that the Queen must perform is to wave to her subjects. When she appears in an open carriage or on the balcony of Buckingham Palace, she acknowledges the cheering crowds with a unique rotation of her wrist. I have tried to imitate this gesture, but couldn't quite get the knack of it, even without a handbag dangling from my elbow. What does she keep in that omnipresent handbag? Breath mints? Pictures of the grand kids? A Harrod's' charge plate? A "Do Now" list ? Might the bag actually contain nothing? Might it be Her Majesty's security blanket? Being in therapy, I notice such things.

According to my supermarket pulp sources, the Queen and her consort have not spent an entire night together since their honeymoon He isn't the one who zips her up in back or who scratches her royal back when it itches. Nor is it he who clasps the strands of pearls around her neck and pins the jeweled brooch to her bosom. It is her lady in waiting. And it is her lady in waiting who sees to it that whenever the Queen travels, a white kid toilet seat goes along and is placed in readiness for the exclusive use of her "royal heine."

Her *annus horribilis* was the year that Elizabeth does not look back upon with pleasure. It was the year that Prince Charles' midnight phone calls to Camilla were made public, the year that Prince Andrew was divorced from Ferggie, and the year that Princess Di went on television and detailed the difficulties of her story book marriage. It was the year that the Queen, wearing a Liberty of London scarf around her head and a Burberry raincoat over her nightgown, stood in the early morning chill and watched Windsor Castle burn.

I longed to console her, to put my arms around her and say, "There, there. It's not so bad. You will get over this "annus horribilis." Things will get better. Take it from me, Liz, I know. I have had some horrible years of my own."

This story appeared in the
New England WRITER'S NETWORK

Home Improvements, 1933

My mother and I are sitting on the top step of the front porch. She is getting a breath of fresh air, and I am looking for something to do on that first morning of the summer vacation. I look up and down the street, hoping that someone will appear who will want to search the gutters of the neighborhood for tin foil or maybe climb Mrs. Weber's tree and steal some cherries. But the street is deserted. I want the organ grinder to appear with his cute little dressed up monkey. I want to go on a picnic. I want my friend, Norma, to come running down the street shouting, "Get on your bathing suit. We're going to Orchard Beach. My mother says you can come, too." But none of this is happening. I am so bored that I consider going down and popping tar bubbles in the road.

I turn to my mother and say, "Tell me how you're going to fix up this house some day when you get that money. When the bank opens again and you can get at daddy's insurance money. Tell me."

Mother sighs and wipes her forehead with the hem of her apron. "Someday talk gets you nowhere," she says. "Someday talk won't get my work done. I can't leave dirty dishes around in this heat."
But I persist. "Tell me anyway, tell me again how dangerous these front steps are."
Mother looks down at the steps, ready as usual, to voice her concern. "Well, these steps are not safe," she says. "They're too steep. That's why you fell down them when you were just starting to walk. What a scare that was. It took five stitches to close the gash on your forehead.." I feel for the scar under my bangs as mother continues. " If anyone gets

hurt on those steps, the mailman, or one of your friends, they could sue me. I always said that these are dangerous steps. And another thing, they are ugly. Brick is what I like for porch steps, not concrete."

" And the front door, that's ugly too, right?"

"Absolutely," says Mother. "That heavy wooden door makes the hall dark. I'd get one of those aluminum combination doors with glass panels and screens that lets in the cool breezes in summer and keeps out the cold in winter."

"And we could build a porch out over the cellar steps, like the Webers did, right? And cook hot dogs out there and toast marshmallows like at a picnic, right?"

"Well," says my mother, "A back porch is nice, but there are a lot more important things than a back porch. Get rid of that old icebox and get a nice new Kelvinator. No more drip pans to empty, no more spoiled food. And some new linoleum for the kitchen floor would be nice. She turns and squints up at the front of the house, at the peeling clapboards. The whole outside of this house could use a good coat of paint, or maybe asbestos shingles. So I'd never have to paint again."

"The porch." I say, "Someday, when you get the insurance money, we'll build a back porch, right? And we'll make hamburgers and hot dogs out there on the porch and toast marshmallows, right?"

But I don't wait for an answer. Norma is coming down the street bouncing a big red beach ball, and I am down those steep front steps two at a time.

The Cabbage

Grandma and I are on the front porch when we hear the cries of the vegetable man coming down the street in his horse drawn wagon.
Tomatoes! Potatoes! Fresh String-a-Beans!

At the corner the driver turns onto Scott Avenue, unaware that a head of cabbage has fallen off his wagon. But grandma saw the cabbage fall and she saw it come to rest in front of the Dolan's driveway. She studies it. "That cabbage is a beauty," she says. For several minutes she continues to appraise it. "It must weigh a good five pounds." She turns to me and gestures toward the cabbage. "Go get it," she says.

I can't believe that she wants me to cross the street and get that cabbage. Kids are roller skating at the far end of the street. Suppose they see me picking a head of cabbage up out of the gutter. Would they think I was stealing it? Would they call me a rag picker, a gutter sniper? I hate that cabbage. I want Mr. Dolan to back his Oldsmobile out of his driveway and smash it. I want a stray dog to come along and pee on it. Shaking my head and squeezing back tears I say, "No! I won't go over and get that cabbage."

"Well, a cabbage does no good there in the street," says grandma. Slowly, because of her bad knee, she gets up from the rocking chair, goes down the porch steps, and crosses the street. Stiffly, because of her bad back, she bends and scoops the cabbage into her apron. She holds her head high as she carries it back knowing, as I do, that from behind her lace curtains, Mrs. Dolan has probably witnessed it all; the cabbage falling from the truck and her Jewish neighbor, my grandmother, crossing over and snatching it up from the gutter. Grandma returns, saying as she enters the house, "What a shame it would be to let a good head of cabbage like this one go to waste."

That night for supper we have holishkes, stuffed cabbage leaves; and the next night we have varnishkes, bow ties mixed with sweet and sour chopped cabbage.

This story appeared in
"The American Depression Cookbook"
Memories and Recipes from the Nineteen-Thirties
Edited by Duane Carr and Pat Carr

What She Did For Love

My grandmother cut out dresses for me on the dining room table. On the same table, and sometimes even at the same time, she stretched out dough for apple strudel and cut up dough into noodles. On sunny days she washed sheets and towels in the bathtub and spread them out to dry on the hedges in the back yard. She sat in a rocking chair on the front porch shelling peas and from time to time, she'd pop a few into my open mouth.

Grandma brought chickens home from the market with the feathers still on and the insides intact. She said that chickens with white feathers were more tender than chickens with brown feathers. If she bought a chicken that was already plucked, how could she be sure what color she was getting? She scooped out the insides over the kitchen sink, naming the parts and holding each one up for me to see; the heart, the stomach, gizzard, intestines, and a little green sack of bile near the liver that had to be removed very carefully because if it broke it would make the chicken so bitter that she would have to throw away the whole chicken. But grandma was careful; she never had to throw away a chicken. After it was plucked and cleaned, she cut it up, placed the parts on a special board, and sprinkled them with kosher salt.

When my mother scolded, grandma held me and rocked me to sleep with Jewish lullabies. She rubbed my chest with Vicks when it was congested and applied mustard plasters that she made from Coleman's powdered mustard. She soothed my bee stings, mosquito bites, and poison ivy with calamine lotion. She powdered me with oatmeal when I itched with measles. She saved the neck of the chicken for me, the marrow from soup bones. And when she went shopping, she bought me blood oranges, halvah, and salty black olives.

Grandma re-strung elastic through the arms and legs of my celluloid dolls, and she made a cradle for my baby doll out of a Quaker Oats cereal box. She saved string and taught me to play cat's cradle. She let me win at Pisha Paysha. And for my amusement, Grandma could peel an apple in one unbroken piece of skin.

Running with Lollipops

My grandfather was always warning me about something. He would say, "Don't sit on the radiator. I tell you this for your own good so you won't get hemorrhoids. And don't sit on the porch steps. Sitting on cement can cause kidney stones and rheumatism. He didn't want me to ruin my eyes by reading in too little light or in bright sunlight. I shouldn't read lying down, in the bathtub, or during a thunder storm. He reminded me to take off my galoshes when I went to the movies so I wouldn't come home with eye strain and a headache. If he caught me picking at a scab on my knee or using a safety pin to remove a splinter from the sole of my foot, he prayed that I shouldn't get blood poisoning.

He warned me not to eat raw, unwashed rhubarb from the garden or green grapes from the arbor. Wild scallions and sour grass were not good either, and I was never to eat what was inside a peach pit. That little inside part was poison. I should not take a lick of anyone's popsicle or ice cream cone. I should not chew on those little orange Chanukah candles, or on tar, chalk, erasers or rubber bands. The more things I kept out of my mouth, the better. There were germs everywhere waiting to enter my body and cause me harm. Never should I sit down at the table without first washing my hands with hot water and Octagon soap.

Grandpa warned me not to drink water from the garden hose or from the bathroom sink. The only water that was safe to drink was from the kitchen faucet. Other things I should not eat were snow, ice from the back of the ice man's truck, milkweed, or red sumac berries. Those berries would cause itching and swelling all over my body. Also, I had to pay attention when I ate watermelon because swallowing a watermelon pit was just asking for appendicitis. Above all,

Grandpa did not want to catch me running with scissors, knives, forks, pencils, or lollipops. I could fall, God forbid, and take out an eye.

"Stop already!" mother said. "Leave her alone. She's just a child and you fill her head with all kinds of crazy fears." And that is when I piped up and asked, "What are hemorrhoids?"

Under a different title this story appeared in the New England WRITERS' NETWORK

A Material Girl

My mother made the dress that I wore on that first day of school. I watched her cut out the material on the dining room table, and I sat on the floor and watched her feet work the treadle of the Singer sewing machine. I was right there when she needed me to wind the bobbin for her or to thread the needle.

Mother dressed me with care for my first day of kindergarten. She said that my hair was so straight and fine that she wished I had a loop on the top of my head like my Patsy doll so she could pull the ribbon through and tie a bow that could not slip off. The bow did not slip off. Mother knotted it so tight that tears came to my eyes.

My teacher's name was Miss Shea. I fell in love with her on the spot when she said, "My, what a pretty dress you're wearing."
I smiled and turned all around, holding out the gathered skirt for her to admire.

"See," I said. "It's rayon taffeta Scotch plaid.
"It's lovely," said Miss Shea.
"Yes," I said. "I know. My mother made it for me."

School Shoes

I wanted to get shoes at the store in our neighborhood that had those cute cardboard figures of Buster Brown and Tighe in the window and gave out free pencil boxes when you bought new school shoes. But grandma took me to the place where she got shoes for herself. She called it an "outlet store." Mostly it was a shoe repair place where Mr. Russo replaced worn out heels and soles. He would shine up shoes that were not claimed after a certain length of time and sell them for "good as new." These were the shoes that Grandma bought for herself. If they were a bit small, they were put on a stretcher and loosened up; if a bit large, a heel cushion was added at the back.

Mr. Russo looked up when we entered the shop and greeted us without turning off the noisy machine that he was working at. "I have something nice for you, " he shouted. "Your size, exactly." Grandma shook her head and pointed to me. "Not for me," she said, "Today I need school shoes for my granddaughter." Mr. Russo turned off the machinery and wiped his hands on his apron. "No problem," he said. "I have something nice for her. I picked up a job lot of school shoes just yesterday." He reached up to a shelf and took down a dusty pair of shoes. He polished each shoe on his sleeve, holding them out for Grandma to admire. He turned one shoe over and drummed his knuckles on the sole. "Real leather." he said, "These shoes will wear like iron."

Grandma examined the shoes. She rapped on the soles approvingly and handed them to me. They were oxfords, brown with dark laces. Nobody in school wore shoes like these. And how did Mr. Russo know my size? He didn't even measure my feet. Grandma held open the half door of the cubby that had a bench and a footstool inside to give you privacy while you waited in your stocking feet for your shoes to be repaired. She told me to sit down and try on the shoes. I kicked off my sneakers and scrunched up my toes, protesting that the shoe was too small. *Couldn't she see that I couldn't even get the stupid shoe on my foot?* But grandma insisted that I push harder. "Walk around and they'll loosen up. You run around barefoot all summer, so it stands to reason your feet are swollen."

"They're her size, all right," said Mr. Russo. "She just has to break them in." He bent down and pressed the toe of each shoe. "See, here's her toe. They're her size, exactly! She just has to get used to them. She'll wear them a couple of times, they'll be perfect." Grandma nodded in agreement. She gave Mr. Russo a couple of bills, and he rang open the cash register and gave her back some coins. He put the shoes in a used brown paper bag and handed the bag to me, but I wouldn't take it. I walked out of the store without the bag, without waiting for grandma.

I wanted new shoes that came in a box. I wanted saddle shoes, or shoes with pink rubber soles. I wanted red pumps. If my new shoes had to be oxfords, I wanted them to be navy blue. I wanted my feet to be measured with one of those sliding things that you're supposed to measure feet with. I wanted a free pencil box like you got at the Buster Brown shoe store.

Holding back tears, I slowed down and waited for grandma to catch up. "I hate these new school shoes. "Hate them! I want saddle shoes like all the girls wear."
"I know," grandma said, "but they're just shoes. You'll wear them out, and next time you'll get shoes you like better. Sooner or later, you'll learn that in this life, you don't always get what you want; at least, not right away."
I took the brown paper bag. I took grandma's hand. And together we walked home.

Party Shoes

All winter long, my family would rummage in a box in the front vestibule where items of winter clothing were kept. Mother would grab a pair of mittens when she shoveled the front steps, and I would wear the same mittens when I went sleigh riding. If it was windy, grandpa would wind a knitted muffler around his neck when he went out to buy his morning paper, and grandma would wear that same muffler later on when she went shopping. We just dug around in the box for whatever we needed at any particular moment. Hats, sweaters, gloves, scarves; all were shared by all.

It was a revelation to me when I found out that in other families, people wore things that belonged to them exclusively. They had their own clothing for special occasions and for different activities. My friend Jessie kept her shoes in a shoe bag on the back of her bedroom closet door. She had school shoes, after school shoes, tennis shoes, ballet slippers, rainy day shoes, snow boots, and shiny black patent leather Mary Jane party shoes. She had white socks with lace around the cuffs that she wore with the Mary Janes. She had white socks with red, white, and blue borders that went with the tennis shoes. All of her socks were neatly paired and rolled in the top drawer of her bureau where she could see at a glance what socks suited the occasion. Never did Jessie wear two different socks at the same time, and never did she have to put cardboard in her shoe because a hole was worn through the sole.

Mother said that Jessie was an only child who had a rich grandmother who owned a big house with a tennis court in the back. She had two parents who worked and earned good money and could afford to spoil her. "Anyway," said mother, "those children don't always do so well later on in life. It's not good for kids to have things handed to them on a silver platter."

But I didn't care how I turned out later on in life.

I just wished with all my heart that someone would hand me a brand new shiny pair of Mary Jane party shoes. On a silver platter.

Skating Shoes

Mother said that she didn't want to catch me clamping roller skates to the soles of my good school shoes. She didn't know it, but my school shoes weren't so good any more. I had cut the sole off the right shoe to keep it from flapping when I walked, and the left shoe had a hole through which I was constantly stubbing my big toe.

"Lift up your feet," mother said. "If you scuffle along like that you will wear out those shoes in no time at all." She shook her head disapprovingly and threw up her hands, complaining to the world in general, "I just can't keep her in shoes!"

All summer long I went without any shoes at all. The soles of my feet were so tough that I could walk on pebbles and hot sidewalks without flinching. But roller skating was different. I hadn't figured out how to roller skate in my bare feet.

Bookmobile

Every other week the bookmobile parked behind the school playground. It was an old school bus painted blue with hinged panels that lifted to reveal shelves with books for children on one side, and books for adults on the other. I could borrow two books for myself on my card and two for my mother on her adult card. Mother didn't have time to pick out her own books. She did piece work at home, embroidering flowers on ladies kimonos. She read late at night even though her eyes were tired because she said that losing herself in a good book helped her to forget her troubles. She wrote down the titles she wanted me to get her: *Oil for the Lamps of China, Anthony Adverse, So Big,, So Red the Rose, Forever Amber*. Or anything by Pearl S. Buck.

I read each of my books four or five times before the bookmobile came around again. It was hard to wait two weeks for new books, so I was always begging mother to tell me about hers. Pointing to a book lying open on the kitchen table with a soup spoon holding her place, I read the title aloud, *The Good Earth*. "What's this one about?"
Mother said, "It's not a book for children. Terrible things happen in this book, things you don't want to know about at your age." But I did want to know, in the worst way. Mother didn't have anyone else to discuss books with, so sooner or later, no matter how busy she was, she relented and told me about the book. The terrible happenings, and all.

She put down the kimono she was embroidering, and said, "*The Good Earth*" takes place in China. There's a famine, and people are starving. They have no food, none at all."
"That's what a famine is, isn't it? No food, nothing to eat?"

"Yes," said mother, "but like I said, "at your age, you don't need to know about things like famines and the killing of babies. There's plenty of time for that."
"Who's killing babies?" I asked. This was something I wanted to know about. My mother continued, explaining that Olan, the Chinese mother, smothered her new-born baby to save it from starving to death, and then she told her husband the baby was still-born. That means born dead."
"I know," I said. "Like aunt Leah's baby, it was still-born."
"Yes," said my mother, "like aunt Leah's baby." I really didn't understand how a baby could be born dead. I just knew that it was something sad that happened in real life as well as in books.

When mother was reading *Gone with the Wind,* she read it in bed in the morning and she propped it against the sugar bowl on the kitchen table when we ate. When I asked what it was about, she summed it up like this: it takes place during the Civil War, down South on a beautiful plantation called Tara, and when Scarlet O'Hara needs a new ball gown, she pulls down the drapes and uses the material to make a new gown because there was a war going on and they couldn't get things like new clothes."

"What else is in the book, what else happens?" I ask. I knew there must be lots more in a book that was so popular we had to reserve it for weeks in advance..
"Well," said mother, "there is a famine in this book, too. Don't forget, there was a war going on and the troops from the North marched through Atlanta, Georgia where Scarlet lived, leaving everything in ruins, leaving hundreds of people starving and homeless. When Scarlet O'Hara looks out on the burned out fields where Tara stood, she swears that as God is her witness, she will never go hungry again."

"And does she, does she ever go hungry again?"
Possibly," said mother, "I haven't finished yet, and you can see what a thick book it is. Lots of things are in store for Scarlet. And let's not forget about Rhett Butler. He's in the book, too. When you are older, you will read *Gone with the Wind* for yourself and find out what happens to them."

I could hardly wait.

B Is for Bellybutton

My first grade friend, Emily, and I are telling each other naughty words. "*Belly*" whispers Emily. She giggles and claps her hands over her mouth.

"Belly isn't a bad word," I say. "My mother says *belly* all the time. She says that my *belly* will hurt if I eat too much ice cream. She says that I'll get a *bellyache* if I gobble my food. Doesn't your mother say that?"

"Actually," says Emily, "My mother says *tummy*. *Tummy* is a nicer word."

It could be that Emily's mother is right. She's Episcopalian. However, Jonah in the *tummy* of the whale? I don't think so. We say Jonah was in the *belly* of the whale. We're Jewish.

I have a sudden thought. "How about *bellybutton*? *Bellybutton's* a good word, isn't it?"

"Well," says Emily, "What you should say is *navel*. That's what my mother calls it."

I thought navel was a kind of orange. But I don't tell Emily. And I don't tell Emily what my grandmother calls my *bellybutton* because I don't want her to tell me that *puppick* is not a nice word. Emily's grandmother is Episcopalian.

Dress Up

When I was a child my fashion models were Shirley Temple and the British royal princesses. They were always pictured perfectly attired for every occasion. Shirley in polka dots and flounces, and Princess Elizabeth and Margaret Rose in double-breasted tweed reefers with velvet collars and leggings. They did not suffer mismatched anklets or missing buttons. Princess Margaret did not appear in Elizabeth's hand-me-down dresses. Shirley did not sing "On The Good Ship Lollypop" wearing the same outfit that she wore when she tap danced up and down the stairs with Bill Robinson.

As for me, I always seemed to be wearing a cast off dress of my sister's that mother had made without a pattern; a dress that invariably drooped at the waist, pulled across the shoulders, or choked at the neckline. Mother dismissed my complaints saying, "Just keep getting "excellents" on your book reports and "outstanding" on your compositions--nobody will notice what you have on."

It was about this time, when I was in the fourth grade, that a cousin, one of my rich relatives who lived in Brooklyn, was struck down by a car that had jumped the curb and killed her, right in front of the brownstone house that her family owned. A few weeks later, we received a large box filled with clothing, mostly brand new, that had belonged to my cousin. There were dresses with smocked bodices and embroidered hems with labels from Lord and Taylor and Saks. There were lace trimmed panties and night gowns that were as pretty as party dresses. There was a pair of red patent leather pumps that you could tell from the soles had never been worn. I tried on a pleated plaid skirt with fringes, held together on the side with a big gold safety pin. I was thrilled. I felt like a princess. But I also felt guilty when I remembered that the girl who had owned these beautiful things had been killed when she was jumping rope on her own sidewalk in front of her own house.

From the bottom of the box, wrapped in tissue paper, I drew out a pair of wrist length white kid gloves. I pushed my fingers into the fingers of each of the gloves, and lovingly smoothed the soft leather against my cheek. I had mittens, and I had woolen gloves, but never had I known the luxury of kid gloves. "Take them off," said mother. "I can't imagine why a child would ever need gloves like these. But who knows, one day they might come in handy."

And one day they did. Wrapped in a white bed sheet, and wearing those white kid gloves, that year I was the most elegantly dressed Halloween ghost in the neighborhood.

The Devines

Miss Devine was nobody's favorite teacher. She didn't like girls and she didn't like boys even more. She didn't like poor spellers or kids who had trouble with fractions. She had no patience with nail biters or fidgeters. She demanded silence and she expected attention. She insisted that you stay inside the lines when you colored.

Hardly anyone remembered a time when the fourth and fifth grades at P.S.11 were not ruled over by the Devine sisters. You had to pass through at least one of their classes, sometimes both, before you went on to Jr. High. Their given names were Margaret and Catherine, but we referred to them descriptively as Fat and Skinny. When you told someone that you were in Miss Devine's class, they would ask, "Which one, Fat? You're lucky. Just pray you don't get Skinny next year. She's mean."

But Skinny liked me. She trusted me to go to the slop sink in the hall closet and change the water in the milk bottle vase that she kept on her desk for branches of forsythia or pussy willows. She had me clean the chalk ledges, wash the blackboards, clap the erasers, and empty the waste paper basket. She said that she let me do these things because I was such a good student, but I knew that for her these were disagreeable tasks that she just didn't want to do herself.

She was always barking out commands. Sit down! Stand up straight! Use your handkerchief! Fold your hands on your desk! Open your notebook! Copy the spelling words from the board! Put down your hand! No! You may not leave the room! I never raised my hand to leave the room. I knew that Miss Devine knew when I didn't have to pee.

Tea Party

Miss Devine tells us that the P.T.A is having a tea party to welcome our new principal. At the party they will serve finger sandwiches. What are finger sandwiches? Anyone? She looks around the room, up and down the aisles. Miss Devine sighs. "Well, finger sandwiches are dainty bite size sandwiches that have the crusts cut off. Bite size, anyone?" No hands are raised. Again, Miss Devine sighs. "Bite size," she explains, "is the amount of sandwich that you can fit into your mouth in a single bite."

She tells us that this tea party is a special occasion, and that everything must be done properly, just so. What the P.T.A. needs are some sugar tongs. These are sugar tongs. She holds up something that looks like a little bent fork with tines on both ends. "See," she says, "you pinch the sides together and pick up a lump of sugar and drop it into your teacup, like this." She picks up a piece of chalk with the tongs and drops it onto the chalk ledge. "Yes, sugar comes in lumps, as well as the loose kind that you sprinkle on your cereal. That kind of sugar is granulated. Lump sugar is the kind they have at tea parties. Ask at home if they have any sugar tongs that we can borrow."

When I get home, I rummage in our kitchen drawer, and finally, triumphantly, I hold up a pair of tarnished sugar tongs for my mother to see. "Are you sure that's what they want ?" mother says. "I didn't think that anyone used lump sugar anymore. Your Aunt Rose gave me those tongs at my wedding shower, but I never had any use for them. When did I ever have time for tea parties?"
She finds a can of Noxon, and watches as I polish up those sugar tongs until they shine like new. "Imagine that!" says mother. "To think I had something the P.T.A needs for their tea party, right here in my kitchen junk drawer."

Playing in Traffic

To me, the flagstones that paved the sidewalks of Glover Avenue were as familiar as pictures in a book. There were lavender slates in front of our house, green in front of Dolan's, and so on, to the end of the block-- pink, blue, gray, rose-- I knew each slate. I knew the scooped out places where puddles formed after a summer rain, and the uneven places where ice developed in winter. I knew where moss would appear and where, year after year, ants would build their sandy mounds. I never got tired of skimming over the smooth surfaces of those colored flagstones on my Union Hardware roller skates.

In front of Dolan's house, the roots of a large old maple tree had lifted up several of the slates, forming a hillock that was daunting to some kids, but was a challenge that I met with ease. I was easily the best skater on the block. Old Mrs. Dolan didn't blame tree roots for breaking up her sidewalk. She knew that kids on roller skates had caused the damage. She finally had to have the broken slates removed, the roots cut back, and the space cemented over. This new surface sent a pleasing vibration up and down my legs when I skated over it. But Mrs. Dolan had not had her sidewalk repaired for my pleasure. She waited behind her front room curtains, and when I glided by, she knocked on the window pane with her wedding band and shouted, "It cost me money to have that sidewalk fixed. Go skate in the road!"

Mother shook her head in disbelief. Imagine telling children to play in traffic! "You tell Mrs. Dolan that your mother doesn't want you to play in the road. It's dangerous! Don't be fresh, just say in a nice way that you are not allowed to skate in the road."

The dangerous traffic that my mother feared, was it Joe Bruno's ice truck lumbering down the street, stopping at every few houses to make a delivery? Was it old Mr. Kleinerman backing his Studebaker out of his driveway at three miles an hour? Or did my mother think that the Bungalow Bar man might suddenly go berserk and send his cute little picket fenced truck careening crazily down the street, bells jingling wildly, and willy-nilly striking down kids on roller skates!

When Mrs. Dolan chased us, the kids yelled back, "You don't own the sidewalk, you old meanie. We can skate where we want to. It's a free country!"
But I wasn't fresh. I just smiled sweetly as I skated by and called out in a nice way, like mother said I should, "I'm not allowed to skate in the road, Mrs. Dolan. It's too dangerous!"

Two In A Tub

As the younger sister, growing up during The Depression in a house where there was never enough of anything to go around, I tried many tactics to get what I wanted. Whenever there was a choice, I would pretend to want the thing that I really did not want. For example, even though black jelly beans were my favorites, I would grab for the red ones. My sister would say that those were what she wanted, and she got first dibs! I pretended to be disappointed with the black jelly beans, the ones that I really wanted. And that was how I got some of my favorite things.

Saying that I wanted the *Superman Comics* got me the *Little Orphan Annie Big-Little Book.* Pretending that I wanted the Betty Boop coloring book, got me the Shirley Temple paper doll cutouts. And never would I have ended up with the chocolate covered cherry from the Whitman Sampler Box of candies if I had not begged for the foil wrapped almond nougat. Later on I learned that this strategy was called reverse psychology, but I figured it out on my own, long before Psych 101, when I was just a child growing up as the younger sister.

It did no good to appeal to my mother to settle claims of unfairness that arose between me and my sister. After the untimely death of our father, mother had all she could do to get food on the table, keep us in shoes, and meet the mortgage payment at the end of the month. If I asked why my sister got something and not me, my mother would say, "Because she's older." And if my sister asked why I got something instead of her, mother would say, "Because she's younger." End of argument.

Once a week my sister and I were bathed together in the same scant tubful of lukewarm water. Hot water was another thing there was never enough of in our house. We got scrubbed and shampooed with Octagon laundry soap, an uncomfortable procedure at best, and my discomfort was intensified by the fact that *I was the one who was made to sit with my back to the faucets.* When my sister pushed me and I cried out in pain, mother would not even look to see if there were red marks on my back. And it did no good to pretend that the water in my end of the tub was warmer. My sister would not change places with me, not even on my birthday.

The unfairness of it drove me to tears as mother attempted to dry me with a towel that was already wet from my sister's rubdown.
"She always gets her way," I sobbed, my eyes stinging with indignation and with Octagon soap suds.
"She's older," said my mother. And, of course, this was true. If my sister and I both lived to be a hundred, I would never catch up. She would always be four years older than I was. She would always get the smooth end of the tub.
"It's not fair," I sobbed, "Not fair."

Brusquely, mother turned me around to face her. "Tell me this," she said, "Where is it written that life is fair?"
And vigorously, she continued to dry me with the wet towel.

Crayolas

Mother says that the walls in this house are thin as paper. On windy nights I lie awake, scared that the whole house will blow away like crumpled sheets of newspaper. A car goes by momentarily lighting up the dark corners of the room. Leaf shadows move across the ceiling. A board creaks, a mouse scurries in the wall. Mother lies on her side of the bed, breathing softly. In the next room grandpa coughs, and grandma calls out in her sleep. I hear the front door open and then I hear it slammed shut. Uncle Robbie is home. The house is safe.

He is in the kitchen banging cupboard doors. He is in the dining room searching for bread in the sideboard. He breaks off chunks from a round loaf of challah. Grandma is always scolding him to use a knife and slice the bread properly. She hides leftovers from him, but Uncle Robbie finds everything; the cholent in an iron pot in the back of the ice box, left over lentil fritters, the last bit of roast chicken. He laughs when Grandma scolds that he should leave something for next time. She wants him to be a mensch, to sit down at the table and eat when everybody eats.

"I need lots of food," says Uncle Robbie. "I'm a growing boy."
"Growing girls live here, too," says Grandma. "Leave something for them, as well."
Robbie laughs and grabs her around the waist. "Let's dance," he says. I would love to see Grandma dance, but she is never ready for such foolishness; she pulls away.

I lie in bed and listen to Uncle Robbie climb the stairs, two at a time. He stops in the bathroom, but doesn't close the door. I hear him pee but I don't hear the toilet flush. Mother gets mad when he forgets to flush. "There are other people living in this house," she says. "Once in a while, think of someone else besides yourself." I listen as Uncle Robbie climbs the narrow attic stairs to his bedroom, two at a time. The floor boards creak as he walks around. One shoe drops, then the other. His bed creaks as he settles into it. Then there is silence.

Uncle Robbie has promised to buy me a Chanukah present when he works at Wellman's hardware store at Christmas time. He asks what I want, "A Flexible Flyer sled? Union Hardware roller skates?" A Schwinn bicycle? But I shake my head. I had learned early on to ask only for things that there was some chance of getting. I tell him that I want the giant size box of Crayolas, a box of twenty five brand new crayons.

I lie awake and color in the leaf patterns on the ceiling with my new crayons that are so sharp that I can do stems and little leaf veins. The wind wraps around the house, rattling the window panes. But I am not afraid. Uncle Robbie is asleep upstairs, and we are safe. The house will not blow away. I fall asleep listening to the wind and thinking about colors. I color the wind magenta.

Sliced White Bread

It was a neighborhood where most of the kids believed that the Jews had killed Jesus Christ.
"They did not!" I shouted.
"Did too!" they shouted back.
"Didn't!"
"Did!"
"Didn't!"

My best friend, Terri Scott went to St. Barnabas Parochial School where the teachers were nuns and the girls wore maroon jackets, navy knee socks, and red and blue plaid skirts that came down below their knees. On Ash Wednesday, Teri had a cross smudged on her forehead with ashes. On Fridays she didn't eat meat because that was the day of the week that Jesus was crucified. During Lent, she had to give up something that she really liked, ice cream, maybe, or chewing gum. Terri made the sign of the cross before jumping in for her turn at Double Dutch, and she kissed the miraculous medal that she wore around her neck before throwing in her potsy. I wondered, was that cheating?

I stayed home from school on the Jewish Holy Days and my mother wrote a note explaining that my absence was due to "religious observance." David Fein and Anna Kotins stayed home on those days, too. We were the kids who were permitted to remain silent at Christmas time when the others sang carols in the auditorium and when they recited the Lord's Prayer. At home grandpa lit little orange Chanukah candles on the milk glass shelf over the kitchen sink. He said that by rights, the candles should be placed in a window for everyone to see, but that we didn't live in that kind of neighborhood. It was the kind of neighborhood where colored lights were strung on trees and holly wreaths were displayed in windows, not menorahs.

When Teri made her first holy communion, she was dressed like a bride. She wore a white veil, white pumps, and white lace gloves. She carried a small prayer book and mother of pearl rosary beads. Now she was required to go to confession and tell the priest the sins that she had committed during the week. Teri worried about sins a lot; venal sins, mortal sins, *original sin*! She said that it might be a sin for her to have me, a Jewish girl, for her best friend. But not to worry, she would recite a few extra Hail Marys, just in case.

I never found out for sure if it was a sin for Teri and me to be best friends. When I entered junior high, I just didn't play with her that much any more. But from time to time, Teri still came to my house for a snack of unsalted butter on Jewish rye bread, and I would go to her house for Ann Paige strawberry jam on Silvercup sliced white bread.

Sunday Visits

My aunts and uncles would drop by unexpectedly on Sunday afternoons. They came unannounced, and mother said that it would be nice if once in a while they came with a piece of cake to go with the coffee that they expected her to make. When she sees them at the door, she makes a hasty survey of what she can put on the table. Grandma's apple strudel is all gone, but there is still some pickled herring, black olives, and an unopened jar of homemade grape jelly. She gives me a few coins and tells me to run to the grocery store for some rolls. Uncle Harry gives me a quarter. He has stomach ulcers and has to watch what he eats. "Here," he says, "get some Uneeda Biscuits. You can keep the change."

They sit around the dining room table eating and talking about the bad things that are happening in Europe and about the bad things that are happening right here, in America. They talk about the Lindbergh kidnapping and about the Sunday morning radio sermons of Father Coughlin.

"He is a very dangerous man," says Uncle Harry, "He blames the Jews for the Depression, for the war, for the banks failing, for everything."
"We don't need a Hitler over here," says Uncle Sammy.
"God forbid," says Grandpa.

They finish the pickled herring. They spread grape jelly on the rolls and drink mother's freshly made coffee. They wonder what the world is coming to.

Grandpa gets my report card and passes it around for everyone to admire. "See, she's the smartest girl in fifth grade," he says.

Uncle Sammy winks at me. "And the prettiest one, too, I bet!" I blush and shrug my shoulders.

Aunt Ray says how tall I am growing. I stop leaning on my elbows and sit up straight.

Aunt Lee sighs and says that she still remembers how heartbreaking it had been to see me, barely two years old, digging in the dirt with a stick at the base of my father's newly unveiled gravestone. She reaches over and pinches my cheek. I pull away.

Why did she always bring that up, about my father's grave? I suck on an olive pit, and wish that it was time for the Jack Benny Radio Show.

Lilacs to Brooklyn

Every spring mother cut branches of lilacs from the bushes in our back yard, wrapped the stems in damp newspaper, and we carried a big, fragrant bunch all the way from Yonkers, where we lived, to the brownstone town house in Brooklyn where Tante Sara lived. We had to take a bus and two trains, each to the end of the line. People smiled at us, enjoying the novelty of flowers in the subway. Even though there were plenty of empty seats, a lady sat down next to us breathing in the fragrance of our flowers with obvious pleasure. Mother broke off a sprig and gave it to her. "From my garden," she said. "Enjoy." I knew that it pleased mother to have lilacs to share with strangers and with our rich relatives in Brooklyn.

When we arrived at Tante's house, she was sitting, as usual, on an upholstered chair near a window in the dining room. She wore a dark dress with lace at the neck and a shiny pin. Her hair was carefully arranged from her weekly visit to the beauty parlor. She wore shoes with straps and her feet rested on a little footstool. According to Mother, Tante sat there like a queen on a throne, never doing a stitch of work, never putting her hands in water. And why not? Mother said that Tante had made an easy life for herself years ago when she arranged a marriage between her beautiful blonde daughter and Mendel, a butcher, an uneducated man who cut up sides of beef and trimmed briskets all day while wearing a blood stained apron and standing inch deep in sawdust. When Tante's daughter had cried and pleaded with her mother not to make her marry Mendel, Tante had insisted. "You will marry Mendel, and one day you will thank me. One day you will be the wife of a very rich man."

And Tante was right. In two years time Mendel owned the shop where he had worked, and it wasn't long before he owned kosher butcher shops all over Brooklyn and the lower East Side of Manhattan. His children attended private schools, and his wife wore diamonds and shopped in the best stores while her chauffeur waited in a Cadillac to help her with her packages and drive her home. Mother called this a story with a happy ending.

Tante motioned for me to come closer. I could smell her perfume, and up close I saw that the pin on her collar had shiny blue stones. She kept looking at me, but she spoke to mother. "Is she a good girl? Is she smart in school? Does she help you around the house?"

"Yes." said Mother, "Yes. She is a very good girl. She helps me all the time, and she is the smartest girl in the class."
"That's what I like to hear," said Tante. She reached into her pocket and handed me two one dollar bills. I looked at mother who nodded for me to take the money.

Tante told the maid to slice a banana for me in a bowl with sour cream and to get some coffee and a Danish for mother. Then she told her to get some meat from the freezer for us to take home. A stainless steel freezer, huge, like the ones that Mendel had in his butcher shops, took up the whole wall between the kitchen and the dining room. The maid showed Tante the meat before wrapping it up for us in pink butcher paper. "That's first cut brisket," said Tante, "for pot roast, and some lamb chops for Papa." Mother flushed. I knew that she didn't like taking things from our rich relatives, but she accepted the meat, even as she had nodded for me to take the two dollar bills. And I knew that she had let Tante pay Sheffield Farms to deliver two quarts of grade A milk to our house every day for a whole year after my father died.

The maid had put our lilacs in a glass bowl that reflected rainbows onto the polished wood of the dining room table. Their fragrance filled the room. In a cage at the window, two canaries flitted and trilled. It was a pleasant scene that I kept picturing during the long ride home on two trains and a bus, each to the last stop. I fingered the dollar bills in my pocket and leaned against Mother trying not to fall asleep. Without the bunch of lilacs, there was nothing special about us, nothing to make people smile at us or want to sit close. We were just two tired people, glad to be going home after taking lilacs to our rich relatives in Brooklyn.

One Sunday Afternoon

Counting back nine months from February, the month in which I was born, I confirm that I was conceived in the month of June. Perhaps it was on a Sunday afternoon after lunch. The dishes were probably unwashed, and the floor unswept. My year old sister was teething and suffering from prickly heat. She had been cranky all morning, and now, unexpectedly, she had fallen asleep in her play pen. Did my father put his arms around my mother and say, as he took the broom from her and stood it in the corner, "Leave that, we'll clean up later. Let's go upstairs." Did my mother smile? Did she let him take her hand and lead her to the stairs? Did she lead him?

Once upstairs, did they tumble onto the unmade bed, and did my mother say, as she kicked the down-filled quilt to the floor, "I have to get out the summer blanket and put this winter stuff away. There's so much to do! Put up the screens, plant the tomatoes, paint the railings. . ."
Did he silence her with a kiss? Did the baby start to cry, and did they hold their breath and listen before they resumed their embrace? Did they pay no attention to the dog scratching at the kitchen door to be let out? Did they ignore the dripping of the bathroom faucet, the buzzing of an insect bumbling against the ceiling?
Did birds sing in the maple trees? Did backyard lilacs perfume the room?
On that long ago Sunday afternoon in June when I was conceived, did the earth move?

And after my sister and I were grown and off on our own, after the dog had died and my parents had moved from the house in the suburbs to an apartment in the city where all the rooms were on the same floor, does my mother look up from her Sunday crossword puzzle to see my father standing in the doorway, smiling shyly, and does he say,
"How about it, do you want to go upstairs?"

Why I Live Over The Moosewood Restaurant

Whenever I happen to mention that I live in Ithaca, New York, invariably someone will ask if I know the Moosewood Restaurant. I say that I do, and explain that the restaurant is on the main floor of the old Ithaca High School building and that I live in one of the converted apartments above. People are always telling me that they went to school here. Just the other day the Fed Ex delivery man told me that my apartment had once been his algebra classroom. He had hated algebra and flunked the regents exam, but he got all teary-eyed when I let him come in and look around. I consider the Moosewood Restauraunt my extended dining room. Whenever I don't feel like cooking, or when unexpected friends drop in, that is where we eat. "How convenient," said my Elderhostel luncheon companion who was seated opposite me. "I ate at the Moosewood once when I visited my niece at college. I still remember how delicious the tofu dumplings were."

This conversation was notable because it took place under a banyan tree at a table in the garden of The Pagoda of Ten Thousand Dumplings in Ganzhou, China. Our guide had told us that here we would get the best dumplings in all of mainland China. Actually, he had said "the best damn dumplings in mainland China." He was gung ho American. He wore a red, white, and blue bandana around his forehead, and he told us Elderhostlers to call him Rambo.
"Listen, Rambo," I said, "If you ever get to the U.S of A, be sure to look me up. I will treat you to some dumplings at the

Moosewood Restaurant which are the best damn dumplings in Ithaca, New York if not in all of mainland America.

The delicious Moosewood aromas that waft up into our apartment eased the period of adjustment for my husband and me when we moved to Ithaca from the Upper West Side of Manhattan, from a block that had a twenty four hour Tex-Mex eatery on one corner and an all night Cuban Szechuan restaurant on the other. I could have followed my nose and found my way home blindfolded. When our son visited us in our new apartment, he greeted us by asking, "What's cooking? It smells great, and I'm starving." We hurried him down to the Moosewood.

After returning home, our son sent us a box of sage scented candles which he said would neutralize the restaurant odors that filter up into our apartment. But we savor those aromas, so much in fact, that I am negotiating with a local candle maker in developing a line of Essence of Moosewood Candles. A few of the scents under consideration are Portuguese Gumbo, Persian Split Pea, and Fennel Frittata.

I have had Moosewood conversations with casual strangers in a noodle shop in Kyoto, in a farmers market in San Fransisco, a kibbutz outside of Haifa, a Posada in Portugal, and in the cookbook section of a Barnes and Noble in a shopping mall in Arizona. A woman who had just bought a copy of *Moosewood Restaurant Low –Fat Favorites* wanted me to autograph it for her when I told her where I live. Though I was flattered and tempted to oblige, in all modesty I declined. I'm not sure that I rate celebrity status simply because I live in Ithaca, New York three flights up over the Moosewood Restaurant.